Unspoken

Truths

Veronica Zamora-Loera, M.A. Ed

DEDICATION

Never forget that you are strong and unique, capable of surviving any struggle. God loves you and He is by your side fighting your battles. Stretch your faith and open your eyes to see that you have never been alone. Make a radical change to transform your life. Know that He is there for you and will never abandon you. He never has and He never will.

To my children, Roxana, Carlos, Lesley, Kennya, Andres, Alexa and Adrian and to my grandchildren, Leo, Jazlynn and Benjamin.

ACKNOWLEDGEMENT

I want to acknowledge those who without knowing my past made an impact in my life. My teachers Mr. Rosado, Mr. Collazo and Mr. Scariano who always pushed me to be my best. For accepting me for who I am and for making me proud of my heritage. To the countless leaders who believed in me; Nancy Voise, Kaye Corrigan, Brian Zallis, Lisa Xagas, Christine Igoe and Marion Friebus-Flaman for their constructive criticism, support and for always making me feel as if I was making a positive impact in our school community. One's calling can never be achieved without the support of others.

To my teachers team at JJHS who were always listening ears to my stories and believed I was a positive influence to my students.

To my friend Rosario (Charo) Santana and Christine Halblander for guiding me with my story and helping me edit and revise it.

To my family for waiting patiently for me while I spent numerous hours editing, revising, restructuring and working on my story while showing me their encouragement and love.

To my mother for teaching me that a woman can do it all. To my sisters Ede, Juana, Faby and Araceli for motivating me to continue my journey as a beginning author and to my son Carlos Lumbreras for using his artistic talent to create the cover page.

Most importantly thank you God for never leaving my side, for rewarding me with a happy life, health, stability and guiding my path back to you when I strayed.

Without you I would not be here. I rest in your promises.

"So do not fear, for I am with you; do not be dismayed, for I am your God.

I will strengthen you and help you;

   I will uphold you with my righteous right hand. "

Isaiah 41:10 NIV

CONTENT

Chapter 1: Growing up

There are things from our past that we attempt to hide from or pretend never happened. We do so to avoid pain and suffering and no matter how successful we become in life, bad memories have the capacity to fold us over and turn us into a river of tears at the mere image of loss, abuse or simply the memory of that overwhelming incapacity to walk away from the bad situation. Terry Crews once said, "Success is the warmest place to hide," I have tried to bury my past and keep it quiet; until now.

We all have a story; our life story...a compilation of events, experiences, and memories. However, people remember in different ways. Some remember their first steps, words, or first mishap. Others recall many beautiful memories about their early years; times of laughter, play, and learning.

After all childhood is a great time in one's life: mom, dad, happy memories. We all desire to live a happy life. No one, no matter what, wakes up wishing for a horrible day.

Here in the United States happiness manifests itself through the American Dream. The drive to have the white-picket-fence lifestyle becomes most individuals' and entire families' ideal. People disregard the inevitable circumstances that life brings and do whatever it takes to achieve the American Dream. I'm not sure if this ideal is the same in every part of the world. I am pretty certain that happiness is everyone's desire, but perhaps not the white-picket-fence lifestyle; especially not where I come from.

I'm from a small town in north Baja California, Mexico. It is currently home to a population of six-hundred twenty three people. I'm not sure if the population there has declined or increased since I moved from there back in 1979.

According to some of my family members, El Ejido is still the same place. It has not progressed beyond paved streets. I have not been back since I left. I plan to be back someday to walk the streets I walked during my childhood to see my old home and the neighborhood I left behind so many moons ago. I want to see the setting just one more time to see if my memories have not deceived me. I am not sure what memories will come back to haunt me. My life there was very traumatic. Presently, I have many negative memories stored about that place, memories that sometimes I wish I did not recall.

For many years, I've had repressed memories about my childhood but throughout my life there have been events that have dug them up.

I now understand that these memories stayed hidden in order to protect me from such an overwhelming past. Inevitably, as I continue to age my memories continue to fade like a foggy day. The child I once was slowly continues to disappear. As this occurs, I continue to strive to become a new and improved person. A person who has learned to live without allowing the past negatively affect her, but at the same time a person that will always remember where she came from. A person who will always keep herself humble, simple, and driven to be a caring and a positive human-being... despite her flaws. I see that as my God given purpose. A duty to help make a positive impact in others' lives. I want to make a difference for those who have suffered through the same experiences I lived through or any other hardship.

Chapter 2: Gaps

Are there gaps in your memories? Missing moments about your childhood, first special gift, holidays? I have many forgotten memories. I have always noticed that I cannot recall many events throughout my life. I was confounded when I noticed the many gaps in my memories. Often, during family conversations, they would tell stories that I had no recollection of. Sometimes, my family would make fun of me and mock me jokingly about having selective memory. However, I was being one-hundred percent honest. I could not recall many things. Contrary to everyone else; they were all able to recall so many more details of past years.

There are many years and events missing from my memories. I have absolutely no recollections of my life before the age of 6. I only remember a few days of schooling after the age of 6 and all these memories come from different times and places. One of my memories comes from first grade at my birth place and others from the time I lived in my mother's hometown near Durango, Mexico. These are all disconnected memories of random days of my life as a child in school.

My brain has erased those years to protect me from knowing about undesired events. No matter how hard I have tried to transport myself to my early childhood, my brain doesn't allow me to recall. I have made up my mind that this occurs for my own protection. I understand now that it is best to stop trying to remember than to remember and relive unnecessary events. Attempting to unveil old memories only to find another horrific repressed memory makes absolutely no sense. It's amazing what our brains can do to protect us.

In the past, remembering has given my life further confusion and sadness. It is for that reason that I have learned to leave the past in the past, repressed memories repressed, and bad memories entombed. I have done this in order to avoid further muddle in my life. Although it is difficult to have many years of my life scattered in my brain, I understand that *if* the purpose for it is to protect me and keep me sane; then I embrace the loss. After all, everything I do remember gives my life meaning and purpose.

Chapter 3: The Water Stream

It may seem contradicting to say that I have very few memories of my early years so I should state it a different way. I have very few *positive* memories of my childhood. On the other hand, I do remember many unfortunate events. Sometimes, I wish I could place those bad memories with the rest of my forgotten memories. Other times, I'm glad I remember. It reminds me of how far I have come from the miserable life I experienced as a child. These memories have made me strong, compassionate, and assertive. I have vivid memories and flashbacks that take me back to chilling and brutal events. I remember the beatings, insults and my mother being brutally abused by my father. I lived terrified of him for many years.

I am dumbfounded about what I can and cannot remember. I don't recall learning to walk, speak, read, or write. Yet, I remember small details, sounds, and vivid images of the abuse my family and I experienced.

My childhood memories begin with one school day, in first grade. It was a clear, warm, wind free day. There was an event at my school; a place with dark lime green paint smeared on cracked concrete walls, and white, rusty window frames that distorted the lime green walls. I remember that day clearly; it is safely stored in my mind.

I had a part in a school play in which I would be holding a boy's hand. I was super nervous, especially because my dad would be a spectator. He was frightening. I remember his piercing eyes watching the play, then nothing else after that. A memory frozen in time.

This particular memory plays in my head over and over again, just like a record that's stuck and skips back to the same part. I *stand on the stage, people watch below and in amongst the crowd a tall, slim and sturdy man watching.* I felt intimidated, scared and awkward to see him standing in the audience. It was traumatizing because if I did something wrong or something not to his approval during the presentation, it would trigger his anger, and I would pay for it with a beating once I got home. After the play no other next day, next week, or next month memory follows at this school.

The images from that day are frozen in time. I see the crowd, my dad, the stage and all of a sudden an empty space where the audience observed. I stand on stage looking at that empty spaces. I see it as a still life in my mind; a fragmented memory about my childhood. What remains clear in my mind are all memories about the abuse we suffered with my father. Violent, repugnant, and unloving situations at the hands of the man that was supposed to love and care for us.

I remember with clarity a day when he dragged my little sister by the hair, standing her up off the eat-in-kitchen chair only to smash her face on the concrete wall because she wouldn't stop crying. I can hear the sound of her skull hitting the wall with a loud *CRACK!* I can still see blood **dripping** down and across her face, staining her old, torn dress. Her forehead was scraped down to the dermis. Dead silence filled the room, seconds later the only sound present in our ears were the sound of our hearts' palpitations invading every cavity of our bodies, like drums playing within us. Then, mother's steps rushing to pick my sister up off the floor and the sound of my father's hand back slapping her across the face to put her in her place. Scenes like these were recurrent. Our short time with him was abundant with the absence of love and compassion. He knew no such things.

Chapter 4: Theories

Throughout my life I have theorized reasons why he abused us. Unfortunately, it is all they are; theories. I don't have any clear answers of why he was so unloving.

I'm not sure if he loved us. He never showed any care, empathy, or sympathy toward any of us. His temper and his reactive ways were always cause for trauma in our lives. All types of abuse against us came from my father's hands. We always felt as if we had to walk on eggshells any time we were around him. Every instant of our existence besides him was uncertain. We didn't know if we would see a new sunrise or if we would take our last breath at his hands.

I wish I could say that I had a normal childhood with loving parents in a safe environment, but that would be a lie. Mom always tried her best to provide for us and she surely cared about our well-being, but my father made no attempt to show any love or affection towards us. The only thing we knew from him was abuse.

It was seven of us; mom, dad, one brother and four sisters; all children under the age of seven. I am the oldest. Due to certain circumstances some of us experienced pain and suffering longer than others under my father's carelessness. Luckily, for my brother and one sister they would be sent away; given as a gift to my maternal grandparents... not sure why, but they were suddenly gone. I often still wonder why he sent them away.

I think of the terror young children feel as they are removed from their mother, siblings, and their home; the only people and place they knew. My grandparents were strangers to us. My siblings were 3 and 4 years old, probably too young to recall, but not too young to suffer through it at that moment. Why did my father decide to send them away? Why did he gift my siblings without hesitation? His actions were contrary to the "typical male"; usually men love their sons. Most aspire to father a boy: not my father. He didn't show any interest or love towards his only son.

In spite of how much he despised the birth of every single one of his daughters, his behavior towards my brother was no different than the way he treated his girls. He lacked love for all of us. He abused all of us.

Throughout my life, I have wondered how my father's actions affected my siblings, nevertheless, I have justified that it was best for them to be away from him. We remained separated from my two siblings for many months. We have never spoken about it. I am not sure if we ever will.

Almost close to a year after my siblings had been sent away, we followed. Not fast enough; unfortunately. Those twelve additional months gave me permanent soul scars, some of which I would carry with me through adulthood. Misery, starvation, all types of abuse; the unthinkable at the hands of the person that was supposed to love and protect us. Conceivably a damaged soul himself; my father.

Chapter 5: My Earthly Father

A tall, 6'2" to be exact, green eyed, light skinned, brown haired, and muscular male; one who never learned to love and care for his own or at least a man that never demonstrated love towards his family. I have questioned many times why we had to endure that kind of suffering. Why were we deserving of that life?

I don't believe there is any justification for abusing another human being. Especially, no justification for abusing children or women. No one has the right to treat another human being poorly; less than a human. Many people that have been abused become abusers, but I believe that everyone has the capacity to turn things around and stop the cycle of abuse. Nothing justifies or excuses a human being from abusing others. So, whether my father experienced a rough childhood himself, his past was not our fault. We were innocent children. He could have chosen to change the cycle of abuse, but instead he chose to treat us worse than animals. I will never know why. He lost his battle with death at the age of 33. He died over 30 years ago.

Although nothing justifies what he did to us. There are some stories that point to why he might have been so abusive. One story narrates that he was abandoned by my grandmother and that he wandered around as an orphan; no mother, no father, no one to protect him, to guide him, or to model for him what a loving family should be like.

On the other hand, there has never been any talk about him having been abused or mistreated by others. However, there is always that possibility, especially when a teen boy is away from his parents, raising himself and wandering around as a loner. Yet, if he was abused it does not justify his behavior towards us. Nothing justifies domestic violence. Nothing justifies child abuse.

Deep inside my being, I know he was capable of being good towards others. In part, because those that had the opportunity to know him personally and spend time with him have shared with me about what a nice and generous person my father was. My mother herself has shared that my father was a very generous, kind, and caring person towards everyone, except towards us.

Before marrying him, my mother saw no red flags about his abusive ways. They 'dated' secretly. My grandfather was very strict; the girls were not allowed to go out much, so dating was done with an antiquated version of texting by using paper and pencil placing it under a rock for the other to find and read. My dad would hide around the corner from mom's house. He snuck over to my mother's front door and place a note for her under a rock. Mom would come out and read it, replied and placed the note under the rock for my dad to come fetch it. That's how it all started.

Despite my mother not seeing any red flags before marrying my dad, she shared that on the day of their wedding my dad said to her, "Congratulations, YOU are now a married woman." "Remember that I am not married, you are." She shared that despite him not being physically abusive in the beginning of their marriage; he never did treat her as his wife in public. My father continued his partying and went everywhere alone. He only took my mother to the theater a couple of times. Mom said, "I loved going to watch movies, so it made me happy to go to the theater with him." "However, he never took me any other place with him." My mother did not see any red flags, but I believe his attitude and his statements to my mother on the day of their wedding were indeed RED flags. She just didn't see it as that at the time. Understanding this and having all those negative memories of him made me want to scream when people share how generous he was towards them, I want to tell them about the person I knew. The cruel and careless person I experienced. The type of father he was.

Other times, I just listen attentively and acknowledge what they have to say. I listen to them hoping I had known the person they knew. Hoping my mother experience the person they describe; feeling jealous of every kind gesture my father shared with them. Perhaps, life taught him the importance of treating others with generosity after he matured. After all, he was only 26 when we moved away from him. Maybe he changed after we parted ways. I will never have answers for all these doubts.

After his death, I heard rumors that pointed to the fact that he never changed. He abused his stepchildren and his new wife. He was nice in public, but a completely different person in private; behind closed doors he was that bad tempered husband and father. I know we need family dialogue; therapy to pull out all the skeletons out of our closets to move on with our lives; healed and renewed, but even after 30 years of him being gone his actions towards us continue to cause uneasiness in our lives or maybe just in my life...

I have lived without questioning any of my doubts for many decades, I recently began to search for answers to clarify some of the doubts I have. This year, one summer night, I had dinner with my mother and for the first time I asked her if my memories were accurate. I wanted to know if what I remembered was true or if what lingers in my mind are distorted memories that hold no truth. Sadly, she confirmed everything to be true. Nothing was a lie or a product of my imagination. It is a verifiable past.

Deep inside, I hoped that she denied my memories. Nevertheless, this was my opportunity to finally get some answers, so I had to accept it. As painful as it was, I had to learn to embrace the truths I remembered. I have always tried to figure out why he was so abusive towards us, so throughout these decades, I formed two theories in my head. The first theory is that my father treated us the way he did because he was treated the same way as a child and he never learned to be loving. He treated us the only way he learned to treat those around him. He learned about life as an orphan wandering the streets, unsafe and lonely, how then could anyone expect him to be caring and loving?

My second theory is that his boxing career left him with brain injuries that caused him to be violent and unaware about how to control his temper. I shared my two theories with my mother that summer night and as soon as I shared with her my first theory; she refuted it. She doesn't believe that he was wicked because he was abused as a child. She promptly interrupted me and said, "No, that is not why he was abusive, but if he was abused no one but him knew about it." "He never mentioned anything about being abused to anyone."

According to my perspective, my first theory still remains an unanswered mystery. Despite my mother being so prompt to discard this theory, she does not have a definite answer for it. She did not live under the same roof with him to give first hand, verifiable evidence of what he experienced. This theory is still a probable reason and cause of his unkind actions.

On the other hand, my second theory is shared with my mother; maybe all the punches to his head during his boxing career affected his brain and he could not control his abusive behavior. She thinks this is the most reasonable cause for his uncontrolled actions. Her answers have not given me clarity to the why of his conduct. Nothing I heard from her that summer night gives me a clear understanding of why my father became the abusive man I experienced. Speaking with my mother gives me peace of mind.

Sadly, I still have bits and pieces of his life, nothing fully concrete, it was good to converse with my mother, but I still have many unanswered questions. Some of which I will never seek answers for... because I am too afraid to ask.

A different version of the narrative about what could have caused my father to be so unloving is a version that comes from several people on my father's side of the family. According to some of his family members, he was "abandoned" by his mother at the age of 13. She moved over a thousand miles away from Durango to Mexicali, Mexico leaving my father alone homeless and motherless. My grandmother *abandoned* him to move away with a new man in her life. Leaving him to raise himself; young and defenseless; just a teen boy.

This abandonment according to his family members traumatized him and molded him to the abusive man he became. However others have a different version. It is said that my grandmother did not abandon him, but instead that my dad did not want to move with her, so after my grandmother's much and unsuccessful insisting to pursue him to move with her, my father stuck to his guns and decided to stay behind. She moved and left my father and his brother at that small town. My grandmother wanted to start a new life with her new partner and her sons did not want to follow her, she felt that leaving them behind was the right thing to do.

She thought they were old enough to stay behind with two families. My mother knows this story because my uncle (my dad's brother) stayed at my mother's house with her family. My father lived with his godfather near my grandparent's home in the same small town. The brothers grew up without a mother or a father, both under the care of "guardians". We will never know what abuse my father was exposed to at the hands of his guardian or by others around him.

I know that his brother had a good life. My maternal grandparents took good care of him. They were kind and caring; they treated him as one their own. My uncle was and still is a wonderful man; always loving and caring; day and night compared to my father.

As for my father, no one has a clear understanding of what that 13 year old boy experienced under his guardian's care (his godfather). There will always be so many unanswered questions. I will always have doubts about his life. However, despite his abusive ways, I will always have compassion for him. For the unknown. Regardless of what he did to us, I often wish he had a happy childhood; a happy life. I hope he never suffered any abuse. My heart aches for him and his situation. I can only imagine how difficult it would be for a teenage boy to live without parents during the most crucial stage of one's life.

A time of change. A time to learn to understand one's feelings and to express intricate emotions. The time to develop empathy for others. A crucial time when parents serve as mentors to guide their children on how to interact with others respectfully, with empathy and understanding. A time for parents to teach their teenage children healthy ways to consider other people's feelings in regards to their actions.

What if my father never had a role model to teach him and guide him towards this understanding? What if he was modeled something entirely different? Something that would mold him to the person he became years later. If he experienced deceitfulness, abuse, or dishonesty from the man that "raised" him, there was no good model for him to follow. How then can he become a loving father?

There are many things that we assimilate to from our past experiences and no matter how hard we try there are things that we *cannot* get away from. Maybe my father was unable to get away from being abusive, because that is what he had assimilated to from his past experiences. Only God knows.

Chapter 6: His Teen Years

Another part of my father's story is that during his youth he was a vagabond...wandering around without direction. He went from job to job and place to place with no one to take him under his/her wing. During his early teen years, he found refuge in boxing. He would later become a popular fighter. He went undefeated for some time. A good, strong middleweight. He taught the town's boys boxing skills. Many people have shared with me what a great boxer he was and that everyone was scared to fight him. He had a boxing ring where all the town boys went to learn from him. He was feared and respected.

This is most of what I know about his youth years. Still inconclusive details. None point to why he would become an abusive adult. I'm sure he suffered, because life as it is brings with it difficulties. What I don't understand is the *why* if he endured suffering he continued the cycle of abuse towards us. I often think about what could have enslaved him to anger and caused him to treat us in such reckless ways.

    We all have the power to choose every day. The power to do good or evil. We were all given free will. His free will was blocked from goodness for many years. There is no other way I can explain it. He had a choice and he chose to abuse his family.

Chapter 7: Beating Gestation

Mom was close to her estimated date of delivery. She was often tired, sore, and pregnant. This time she was pregnant with her fifth child. The last child she would share with my father. She was home with my sister and me... hungry and moneyless; nothing different. We had not eaten for days, so she decided to cook a couple of eggs to feed us. We had no food in the house, except for two baskets full of eggs. The problem was that they belonged to my father and he had prohibited my mother from touching any of the eggs from *his* two baskets. He had labeled the two baskets. One labeled *'gallinas finas'* (good quality eggs) and the other *'gallinas corrientes'* (generic eggs).

My father had fighting roosters which he fed more than he fed his family. The eggs in the *gallinas corrientes* basket were the roosters' food. He fed them the egg yolks to prepare them for fighting. They needed a nutritious meal to be strong and ready for each battle. The eggs from the *gallinas finas* were eggs that he attempted to hatch to have strong fighting roosters. You may be asking yourself, why someone would have eggs that he wants to hatch in a basket? I'm not sure either, but he did. Not only did he label them, but he also counted every egg to make sure none went missing. We consistently went without food, but that was not a concern of his. We often missed meals for days at a time and mom tried to gather food, but with no money it was impossible.

The day came when she could no longer tolerate seeing us hungry. Mom had to do what she had to do to keep us alive. She simply couldn't take it anymore, seeing us hungry broke her. She did what every caring mother would do, she took two eggs from one of the baskets and hurried to cook them before my father would come home.

She always avoided cooking the roster's food at all cost. However, knowing that we had not eaten for days pushed her to the edge. Any other time, she avoided cooking the eggs, not because she was a weak woman but because she was terrified of my father's reaction. I remember her praying; asking God that my father would not show up and catch us eating the eggs. Regrettably, what she feared the most happened. Her prayers were not answered. In spite of the fact that he never came home around the time she decided to cook the eggs… talk about bad luck, he came home early that day. "Sniffing like a cat" my mother has shared.

Exasperated he walked towards the small kitchen and inspected the egg shells. He frantically counted the eggs in both baskets. Sadly, mom had grabbed two of the *gallinas finas* (good quality) eggs to feed us. Why was she so careless? I wondered for years. What if grabbing eggs from the other basket would have prevented her from such an unmerciful beating? Deep down, I knew she would have suffered the same consequence regardless of which egg basket she had chosen the eggs from. I still wonder anyway. I wonder if that would have made a difference. I did not eat eggs for many years. I still can't eat egg yolks, I'm not sure if it is due to this memory and the abuse mom experienced for feeding us eggs that day. I just can't eat them.

I have tried to get over it for many, many years, but I replay this scene with clarity in my mind over and over again. My brain has instant replay of all these memories. They come like flashbacks; I recall *the stomping of his feet on the concrete floor shaking*

our fragile bodies as he walked out of the kitchen and

towards us. I remember mom attempting to protect

herself, raising her hands up to her face as a

protective shield. I can see her as she braced for

impact. His leg swung with force and landed on her

back, pushing her abruptly against the wall; her belly

bouncing off the cold, hard, concrete. Then again, his

feet crashing on her body repeatedly, with no remorse

or compassion for her or the unborn baby. I can see

her falling to the ground onto her knees and him

pulling her back up on her feet by her long, dense

hair; only to kick her back down to the floor over and

over again. Finally, a blow to her bottom bruised her

coccyx and placed her in bed rest for many days.

After that horrible incident, day after day, she laid painfully on the wooden cot. She turned herself at a snail's pace from one side to the other, pushing herself with her hands and unable to use her legs to readjust her position to relieve her pain. Her big belly didn't help the situation either. She suffered more than I had ever seen her suffer before. Several days after that brutal beating, my uncle came to visit from Tijuana as he occasionally did. My father took me outside with him to greet his brother. My uncle knew mother was close to her delivery date, so as it was expected; he asked my father where she was. "She is not feeling well." my father said as he gazed at me with a "*you better shut-up look*." I knew better; I said nothing.

I could sense that my uncle suspected something was wrong, but he left without further questioning. I tried to ask him for help by blinking repeatedly, but he missed my signal. My effort went unnoticed. My plea for help was unanswered.

My father had refused to let him into the house to avoid my uncle's suspicion to be proven correct. He told him that mom was sleeping, because she was tired. I wanted him to know that she was hurt and unable to walk, but it was probably best that he left without knowing. A few days later mom delivered a healthy baby girl. My dad showed up to the delivery long enough to find out the baby's gender. When he found out it was another girl, he was disappointed. *"Otra pinche vieja."* he mumbled. Then, he walked out not to be seen for days.

He hung out at the corner bar; usually with two lewd women by his side. None of them as beautiful as my mother, yet they seemed to make him happy. At least happier than he looked around us. How ironic...it made me sad to see him smiling and laughing as he walked down the street accompanied by those women. "Why wasn't he happy and smiley around us?" I wondered.

Chapter 8: Back to Work

Not long after mom delivered my baby sister, she was back to sewing and ironing clothes for people around town. She limped her way around to do her work. It was hard for her because not only had she just delivered a baby but her coccyx was still injured. It took a long time to heal. She eventually did. She had no permanent, physical damage. However, I know that she also carries deep soul scars to this day. I can see it in her eyes.

She has always been a hardworking woman. In the past, her ironing and sewing was impractical at times, because despite all her hard work...her effort was pointless because she worked and my father took her money to continue his partying. It was best for all of us when he was gone. It was terrible when he came around just to take mom's hard earned money to drink and party away while we were abandoned and hungry. She did her best to provide for us, but without his help, it was difficult; nearly impossible. I will never understand why if he didn't help us, he took from her. Taking money away from my mother meant taking food from us; as well as our hope and comfort. I would see her slaving herself away, sewing and ironing crisp, straight lines onto pants and pleated skirts to earn a few pesos to better our situation. Then, my father bullying her by taking her money.

She work with such dedication and passion. She laid all of the clothes on the cots to sort them out before she delivered them clean and perfectly ironed to our affluent neighbors. My mother has always been talented. She has sewn clothes since her early teenage years and continues to sew currently. Her talent helped us when we needed it most. We were 'well' as long as my father wasn't around to take her earnings.

She has used her trade to support us. It was her sewing that helped us progress. After we left my father's side, she continued to work as a seamstress to provide a better life for us. I will never understand why my father didn't appreciate her. He was lucky to have her as his wife; beautiful, hardworking, and talented. Some things have no explanation. This is one of them. There are many things I will never understand or find answers to; his ways, his lack of compassion, his inability to love and care for us. The abuse.

Chapter 9: An Eternity

This way of life continued for many months after my siblings moved away with my maternal grandparents. Three of us remained in hell close to one more year.

I have always known that our suffering was not mother's fault. She was terrified, helpless, and with no one to support her. I wondered why almost no one helped us. We lived around my dad's family; three of his sisters and his mother. Two of my aunts lived in poverty as we did and the other lived well.

Our 'rich' aunt was not careless about us, she probably ignored our situation. My grandmother was the only one who always worried about us. She would take a little flour from one of my aunts, sugar from the other, and she would bring it to my mother. With the items grandma brought mom, she made the most wonderful flour tortillas. We loved flour tortillas. We still do. During my childhood eating flour tortillas after days without food was amazing; tortillas were our filet mignon.

One special night grandma brought us a few potatoes, flour and some vegetables from my aunts' pantries; mom cooked the best meal ever. The aroma of grilled onions, tomato and diced potatoes filled our nostrils. I still like the scent of potatoes and grilled onions. I cook potatoes just like mom did and the scent transports me back to that old setting.

On that particular day, we waited impatiently for our long deserved dinner. She was just about to serve us dinner when my dad and two of his friends showed up. He often brought friends to our home. He did again that night. Mom promptly sent us to our cot as my father demanded for her to serve dinner for him and his friends. We waited there for what seemed a very long time. The smell of the food must have clogged my mind because I took a leap of faith. I walked into the eat-in-kitchen and asked, "Are you friends going to leave some food for us?" My mother rushed me back to the cot and shushed me. Moments later his friends walked out and hell broke loose. He smashed my face on the cot and dashed passed me to grab mom by the hair. He yanked, screamed, kicked, punched, and swore at her. "You should teach them some manners." he said. Then as if nothing had happened he laid in his cot and fell asleep instantly. He snored like a bear. How could his conscious allow him to rest? It did!

He never showed any remorse or shame. As I mentioned before all those punches to his head damaged his brain and made him violent or maybe it was something in his past that traumatized him and caused him to treat us the way he did. Everyone that remembers him always say, "He was a tough guy." He was nicknamed; bellicose. In my mother's town everyone knew us as Bellicose' daughters. Despite his nickname too many remember him as a kind and generous man. "He would take his shirt off for anyone," shared Juan (my cousin's husband).

For years, many of his family members have continued to share stories about his generosity. They have always found an opportunity to announce how nice my father was, it seemed as if they wanted to push this information down our throats. Sometimes, it rubbed me the wrong way and I would excuse myself and leave the conversation. Other times, I would listen patiently while thinking; I wish I would have experienced the man they did. I never did and I never will. At least not during this lifetime.

Growing up, all I knew was his cruelness. It was great when we could be away from him. This occurred either when he would disappear to continue his partying or when we went to work in the fields. We went to work with *abuelita*. She took us to work with her *a la pisca* to the cotton fields. It was hard work, but grandma needed the money and we were happy to accompany her. At the cotton fields we were paid according to the weight of the cotton we collected. I remember grandma lifting my sister and me to push down on the cotton sack to make it as compact as possible and get a couple more pesos for the day.

Although, work at the fields was not easy, it was better than being home when he was around. The cotton bolls' sharpness were no match for his striking feet. The puncturing of the bolls' spikes between our fingernails were torture, but nothing compared to the blows my father took at our already bruised bodies.

My small, fragile frame was battered and sore all the time. There was no mercy, no holding back, his rage was never ending. His compassion was non-existent. I refer to these years as the most colorful years of my life. During this time the bruising on my legs, arms and dorsal had no time for healing. I had different shades of red, blue, purple, lime green, and yellow fading off my body at all times. The discoloration on my legs, arms, and my sagittal planes remained for many months. Despite this, I never thought about ever leaving my home, it was the only place I knew. I never expected that our stay there would come to an end. It did. My last day at the torture house was the day I walked away and never looked back. We left so unexpectedly; no planning, no packing. We had nothing to take with us, so we just left.

We disappeared into the horizon to find a new beginning far away from him. Alexander Graham Bell once said, "When one door closes, another opens." Sometimes the door that opens is no better than the one that just closed, but I have learned that every experience is a learning opportunity. A strange way that life uses to strengthen our characters." That's how I see all my experiences. They are all learning opportunities that have formed the person I've become. For many years, I had forgotten the reason for which my parents argued; the reason for why we left. Unfortunately, I remembered. It's been almost 40 years since we moved from there, perhaps someday I will go back to find closure, but for now I will just continue to work on healing.

Chapter 10: The Straw that Broke the Camel's Back

The reason why we left my father's side was a blur for many, many years. I remember that we left after mom and dad had a big argument. A different kind of argument. One where mom spoke up and stood straight across from my father screaming at him and defending herself. It was definitely different. Mom never won any of their arguments. She won this one; the first and last one.

It was the only time she had screamed at him and the only time he did not beaten her for doing so. I remember seeing their faces so close to each other as I peeked out the open window space. Their faces were so close to one another that I could see their saliva flying back and forth as they yelled at each other. Mom came back inside the house crying and with a strange expression on her face. It was an expression of fear, anger, despair; different mixed emotions. After the argument, father left for the night as he often did and mom cried herself to sleep that night like many other nights. The next morning, he showed up early with a large amount of money and handed it to mom. It was the price he would pay for one of the biggest mistake of his life.

Later that morning, a car picked us up and we drove off to a new beginning…as we drove down the dusty, narrow, unpaved street; as we departed to never return, I decided to wave goodbye to my father who was playing at the baseball field on the right side of that same road. I remember the panic in mother's eyes and her desperate attempt to push me down away from the car's window to avoid eye contact with him. She feared that he would follow us and hold us back; forcing us to stay. But he didn't. He very casually waved back.

Chapter 11: Bad Harvest

We continued down that dusty, narrow road and after a long car ride we arrived at a bus station. I don't think I had been there before. If I had been there, I had no recollection of it. Once there, we had to wait for what seemed a long time. While we waited mom paced back and forth, cracking her knuckles and looking around to inspect every angle of the bus station. She wanted to make sure my father had not followed us there.

After a while, we finally boarded the bus. We had absolutely no luggage just a plastic bag mom carried with a couple of items and important documents, nothing else. She had her hands full with an eight month old, a four year old, and me (almost seven years old). We left with just our shirts on our backs.

Once the bus drove off, mom continued to look around. She kept checking every car that passed us and drove in the same direction as the bus. I'm not sure if she slept. She was vigilant. Every time I looked at her, she was looking out the window scanning every car that came close to the bus.

The bus ride was longer than the car ride. Eventually, it turned dark and we fell asleep. This lasted another day or two. I don't remember getting off the bus at any point before arriving at mom's old home. We travelled on the bus from night to day, day to night. We arrived at mother's hometown to her parents' home after three days or so. The bus stopped at a corner very close to my grandparents' home. Their home was a large place with multiple bedrooms, a large patio filled with fruit trees; apricots, figs and blackberries, a corral with livestock, and a fence made out of sun-dried brick, clay and straw; adobe. A safe haven not for long.

It's a small town called La Joya, there my grandparents lived off the land. They owned acres and acres of fertile land. They planted beans and corn every year. Harvest was not always good. The year prior to our arrival had been a good farming season. My grandfather was still marketing the harvest the first few months after our arrival. He had a large two floors room on the southwest side of the house; a 25 by 20 by 20 feet filled with corn from top to bottom. There were no air bubbles in the entire room. The land had been good. It had provided enough corn for papa to sell and enough to feed us.

Unfortunately, we weren't so lucky the following harvest season. A drought had damaged all the crops. Money was tight and with five new mouths to feed; times were tough. Papa told mom she had to leave and go north to the United States. "You are our only hope for survival." he said. My mother was hesitant and scared. "What about my kids?" she asked. "We will take care of them." "Don't you worry about them." "We will all be well." Papa continued.

He gave my mother no choice. He told her she *had* to leave and send money to Mexico for us to survive. It was as difficult for her as it was for us to be apart from each other. She has shared how difficult it was for her to start a new life away from us. She worked hard and made sure to sent her parents money every week. She knew how difficult it was for us in México, so she limited her spending and sent us as much as possible. She kept $20 dollars for herself from each pay check, except the week she had to pay rent. She sent the rest to us every week.

During her time away, grandma made sure she kept mom informed. She shared with her every little detail, sometimes adding little fibs that worried mom. She was never at ease about being apart from us. Inevitably, she had to endure being on her own to provide us with a better future and honor papa's request. She loved her father and respected his decisions.

Chapter 12: Traveling North

No goodbye, no kiss, no so longs, suddenly one night, mom left. We woke up to an empty bed. She was gone. We were orphans. Sure, we had mama and papa, but mom and dad were long gone. Not long after she left we began to receive dollars from the United States.

The money she sent was not only to help her parents but it was money to help them raise us. She sent enough money to feed us and clothe us. Despite that, we continued to live very humbly. We ate tortillas, beans and soup almost every day. Nothing fancy but at least we had a meal every day. We probably had better meals than that we have now. Everything was organic. We had apricots, figs, blackberries freshly cut from the trees, corn tortillas made from scratch, and fresh beans from the harvest.

Mama boiled corn to make the fresh cornmeal to make tortillas. We did help with the hard work, we carried a heavy 5 gallon bucket filled with boiled corn to take to the mill to mix into the texture we needed to make the fresh tortillas. At my granparents' town we also got to eat meat once in a while.

At the small town the butcher only sold meat on Sundays; chicken and beef shank. They only sold limited quantities, so people had to get there early enough to purchase the meat. Our grandparents attended 5am Sunday mass, so we usually had the opportunity to eat meat once a week. When I say that we got to eat meat once in a while, it was not only because of food shortage, but more so, because of the inequitable treatment from mama towards us.

As you may recall, two of my siblings had gone to live with mama and papa before my sisters and me, well, my sister and I were not as lucky as our other siblings to eat meat weekly. We were lucky if we had it once a month. You see, our lives with our grandparents were not our happily ever after. Since we came into the family months after my other siblings, we were not well-liked by grandma. Papa was neutral. Unfortunately, with grandma things were unfair. We received different treatment. We were the orphans; los arrimados (the freeloaders).

　　As we gathered at the small kitchen table to eat, we were served different meals than my other two siblings. We were served rice, vegetables, and beef or chicken broth. While my other siblings were served meat on their plates, we could only get meat once we finished what was already on our plates. Sometimes we would just get beans, depending on whether or not we had been 'good' all week.

I'm the oldest of the five siblings, so I noticed the different treatment. I began to speak up and grandma didn't like it, so she began to complain to my mother. I was seen as evil: a trouble maker. I was the black sheep of the family. The rebel. The mouthy one. I recall telling my grandmother, "My mother sends money so that you feed us equally, not just some of us. You are not fair." She would always act out a scene after I made her angry. She would pretend to pass out as she fell into her bed, she would ask for water. My sister would bring her a glass of water every time. She would spill it on the floor, as she let her arms go limp. She would then regain her composure after a few minutes and I felt very guilty every time. I always feared that I would cause her a heart attack or something similar. It would scare me enough to keep my mouth shut for a while, but sooner than later, I would complain again. Mom shared years later, that grandma wrote her many letters complaining about me. Mom knew her well, so she began to save money to reunite us with her.

Although, in the beginning of our arrival to my grandparents' house life there was not as bad as living with my father; it would soon take a turn for the worse. I was only seven years old, but that did not stop a couple of neighbors (brothers) from pulling me into an abandoned terrain to sexually abuse me. I was fondled and they relieved themselves. I still don't understand how they could do that to a child. It went on for over a year. It became a routine that made me feel soulless. That's the only way I can explain it. I have never told anyone about this; not my mother, my sisters, or friends. I'm guessing it is time to take the weight off my shoulders. I remember being taken into the abandoned lot, behind a large adobe building;

land filled with dried up weeds and random cactuses. I was always cornered against a wall with my face pushed against it. I can still feel their breath on my neck and their rough hands pulling my panties down. It gives me goose bumps. I am not sure if they told each other about the abuse, because they performed the same act on me every time.

I remember their hands touching my personal places and their privates rubbing against my buttocks. I was just a little twig. How could they be aroused by a child's nude body? I can only partially understand it now; they were sick pedophiles. They were horny teenagers looking to relieve themselves any way they could, with any victim they could find; any innocent, helpless victim for their cowardly acts.

I am not sure how many times this happened and I have their faces blocked from my memory. I do, however, remember their skin color and body frames. I am not sure why I can still see them as shadow, phantom-like frames in my memories. I hope to never see them in person again. Although, I don't hate them and I have forgiven them, the thought of seeing them puts me in a state of uneasiness. I feel embarrassed and I don't know why, and although I know their actions were not my fault; feeling that way is inevitable.

It is hard to erase these memories off my mind. I have tried to forget about them just as I have forgotten many awful things that happened to me, but they too are vivid memories in my restless mind. I still have nightmares about them occasionally. I wake up scared and I can sense the fear I experienced back when I was 7. The fear disappears when I realize it was just a bad dream. I've have had the same dream over and over again. Sometimes in my dreams, it is my children that are in that situation. That is scarier than going back to my own past reality. These are simply, terrible nightmares!

It is due to this, that I have never trusted anyone around my children. I'm sure no one would blame me for it, if they knew my story. Mistrust has held me hostage for many years. Due to these shadows from my past, I have doubted everyone for many years. I know my kids are blessed with good, and "normal" parents; not perfect beings but loving and caring people. Unlike me, they have two parents to protect them and look after their well-being. It was hard to live as an "orphan" when mom went north and dad stayed behind, so I want to be there for my own children, always.

I never want my kids to be without the assurance that we will be there for them in every situation. For me, growing up was hard so my priority in life is to provide them with the best life possible. It was hard not to have someone to take us under their wings and care for us with unconditional love. Mom was the only person that loved us no matter what, but when mom had to leave, everything changed. We had no one who truly cared about our well-being; our social-emotional or psychological being. I never felt welcomed in anybody's home and certainly never felt pure love.

There was one place, in particular, that we visited often: an aunt's home; a spotless, well organized place. A large ranch home with many rooms, a corral for their livestock, and many cousins. Their beds were always very neatly made, decorated with fluffy pillows with their brand new, unplayed with dolls sitting in the middle of the perfectly arranged bedding. My aunt saw us as the dirty, lice infested kids. Too dirty to lay in their beds; too dirty for a sleepover. There, we were usually fed leftovers. Perhaps not intentionally, because my aunt had to make sure she had enough to feed her own children before feeding us. I am not being ungrateful; I'm just stating the facts. One thing was for sure, my sister and I had to wash the pile of dirty dishes; every time. After all, we were the orphans and she was doing us a favor. It wasn't her responsibility to feed us or take care of us. However, she could have been kinder than she was, we needed to feel loved and no one truly demonstrated that sentiment towards us. I did, however, understand that it was only right that we helped out with the chores after receiving a meal all things considered, I don't think her plan was to make our lives miserable, but her actions towards us sure did not help improve our status quo.

It was at her house that I experienced an event that has not abandoned my memory nor left my thoughts for decades. I would drool over the thought of showering in their bathroom. I had never seen a shower before, so I was thrilled over the possibility of showering there. Regrettably, when I asked my aunt (timidly) and with some hesitation if I could shower with my cousins (girls) her response was, "No, because you are too sneaky and slick!" "Fisgona y mañosa sound much more impactful in Spanish." These words have a sexual connotation. I must have done something wrong or exhibited sexual behavior to trigger the way she responded to my question. If I showed signs of sexuality, it was due to what I went through with my abusers during my childhood. I didn't mean to do bad things, I don't recall if I ever did. There is no other way she would feel that way about me, no other way she could judge me to that degree.

What else would justify my aunt's comment about me being "fisgona and mañosa?" I will never forget she said that to me or about me. It has hurt me for years. It still bothers me deep down, but I have no bad feelings towards her. It did, however, create more confusion in my mind.

As an adult, I have learned that it is just the way she is. No filter and no bad intention, just her personality. In the present, there have been times when I felt the urge to ask her why she said that about me, but I always deter from it. The words get stuck at the tip of my tongue. I produce absolutely no sound. This is why, I have not confronted her or said anything to her about it.

After all, despite the rough treatment towards us, she fed us every time we visited. Her roughness is just her personality; harsh, opinionated and outspoken. No hard feelings remain, just a sorrow deep down from the lack of understanding of the why she denied a child from poverty (a seven year old) a dream. A simple act of kindness that would have made me euphoric just by allowing me to experience a shower.

I have forgiven her, so I will never confront or ask her about it. Doing so would make her feel bad and forgiveness includes letting go and not bringing it up again. Letting go has also helped me to feel at ease and not feel anger in my heart for something that happened such a long time ago. The past is the past and it belongs in the past, therefore, I had to let go. I have not forgotten about it, but I do not dwell on it. I have peace in my heart and mind about the situation. I

have moved on.

Chapter 13: The Fields

That same year, at the age of 8, I began to work in the fields during the summer once more. This time, I worked picking beans with two landowners; my uncle and a neighbor. My uncle was a good man. He drove us to work every day to the pitch black fields before sunrise in order to begin work before the sun was blazing down at us. We worked 6 to 7 hours straight. We took a break at noon to eat in a small groups around a campfire. We had pewter cookware that my uncle used to heat up our food in. It was the best food in the world. A good meal after a hard day's work. When lunch was over, we went back to work until the sun begin to set and we could no longer see clearly. It was hard work; we worked from sunrise to sunset but I enjoyed it. I remember the sun's glare blinding me and burning my skin to a bright red the first weeks, then my skin turned leathery brown after a few days. However, I enjoyed the ride back home on the back of the pickup truck as my ashy blonde hair danced with the air that soothed the burning on my skin. It was a fun highlight of my childhood.

I worked with my uncle and his family for about four weeks, from the beginning of June and until the start of July. Once we were done picking the beans in his fields, I started working with my grandparents' next door neighbor. Working with my uncle was hard, but fun.

On the other hand, working for the neighbor brings back bad memories. He was an older man (my grandpa's age), I'm not sure how old. He was probably in his late 50s, early 60s. I was 8. He swung by the fields throughout the day and occasionally spanked me with bad intentions. He wanted to feel my private parts. I remember clearly, the day he scooped me off the ground with a tight grip as his hand pressed down against my vagina. Nasty old man! Thankfully, it never went beyond that, but even as I write this remembering his actions disgust me. It makes me nauseous to remember his actions. My life was surrounded by pedophiles; dirty and nasty men. I never confronted him about it, nor told anyone about his violation against me.

I went back to that town at age 16, luckily I never saw him. I don't know if I would have said anything to him if I saw him while I was there. It was probably best that he was not around. I was still too young to plan a confrontation. He was an adult, I am sure he knew that what he had done to me was inappropriate.

I have not been back to that town, it has almost been 30 years now. Many years after my last visit, I found out he had passed away. I remember feeling relieved when I learned of his death. Feeling that way still makes me feel guilty. He was part of making La Joya a hell hole to live in, yet he was someone's father, grandfather; family member. I am sure someone loved him.

I do, however, often wonder how many other children suffered the same faith under his supervision. How many of them were abused? How many of them are still quiet? Hopefully, none. Hopefully, there are no victims and if there are, I hope they have all found peace and forgiveness in their heart to move on and live a healthy and normal life.

Chapter 14: Following Mom

Thank God that all things come to an end because the day came to leave yet another hell hole. Finally, mom sent for us. My memories are crossed about my first departure to the United States, but I remember riding the train from somewhere in Texas to Chicago's Union Station. My mom's only brother travelled with us. He would take us to reunite with our mother. I remember being scared about crossing the border from Mexico to the United States. I understood the concept of being undocumented at such an early age. I heard my family members talk about *la migra,* so I was scared. My brother was born in the United States and my uncle had been granted a visa (green card), so I was the only one traveling undocumented.

Coming here was the beginning of a new life, still a scary change for me and my brother because we had to acclimate to a new way of life, new customs, and a different language. There were so many mixed emotions, yet it was a new start to our lives--A life with our mother.

Once we arrived at Chicago, the hardest part became not speaking the language and worrying that immigration could deport us any day at any time and send us back to a life of uncertainty. We lived in constant fear, but at the same time, we lived better than we had lived ever before. It was the calm before the storm. My brother and I devoured food desperately. We went through bags of oranges. Mom was very understanding with us, she knew we had been deprived from food for a long time, so she allowed us to eat as much as we wanted. She was in awe about how fast we went through groceries. It was a great new beginning, not only did we have food and shelter but most amazingly for me was that one of my dreams would come to pass. I was finally able to shower in a bathroom better than the one my aunt had denied me months before.

I was finally able to shower as I had once dreamed. We had a bathroom with a huge tub. My brother and I sat in the bathtub until our skin was white and wrinkly. We looked like prunes. We sat in the bathtub for hours. Splash, splashing every day, twice or three times a day. It was amazing. It's ironic how life's simple things are taken for granted by many and seen as a dream by others. My dream had come true, I was able to shower. A privilege we should learn to appreciate always; water.

We celebrated our first New Year in Chicago, it was January 1981, I would soon be 9. I was very happy to live in a safe place with mom. Everything was perfect despite having constant fear of going outside and getting caught by immigration... everything else was peachy.

We lived across from a park filled with see-saws, swings, and slides. Unfortunately, we could only enjoy them visually. We could only enjoy the view from our third floor window. Mom asked us to stay inside all day, and not open the door to anyone. We obeyed.

Soon after we arrived, our lives were beginning to fall into place. We began attending school shortly after arriving. My brother and I both attended the same multi-grade bilingual classroom with one of the best teachers in the world; a firm, but compassionate Mexican man. One who appreciated our good manners and our first language; he used us as an example of good behavior. After all, we were well trained in the Mexican educational system. An educational system that used corporal punishment for bad behavior. A place where every single student would rise to their feet and in chorus greeted every adult that walked into the classroom. A place where children waited for the adults' hand signal or verbal praise before sitting back down. I remember very few things about my schooling in La Joya, enough to remember being hit by a ruler on both sides of my hands, because no one admitted to having stolen a classmate's eraser. I know, for some reason, I always remember the bad stuff.

According to Stanford University's Professor Nass, "The brain handles positive and negative information in different hemispheres." "Negative emotions generally involve more thinking, and the information is processed more thoroughly than positive ones. We tend to ruminate more about unpleasant events and use stronger words to describe them--than happy ones." That explains why I remember the bad experiences so vividly.

Attending a new school in Chicago was difficult. Despite Mr. Rosado using us as good examples of behavior; acclimating was difficult. I had some embarrassing and bad times at the expense of other students in my class. Our classmates laughed at us every time we would stand up to greet the adults that entered our classroom. Mr. Rosado would shush them and always gave them a speech about how they should follow our lead and learn about true respect. He built my self-esteem.

He also transitioned me into speaking, reading, writing and listening to the English language promptly. By the time I was in 4th grade, I was able and safely. We stayed at a hotel for a day and mom bought Greyhound tickets from Texas to Illinois. Another bus ride to a fresh start. This time, three females on the road to prosperity accompanied by a young man.

Chapter 16: Again and Again

Once we were back in Chicago, our living arrangements changed. We moved into a new apartment building on 26th Street and St. Louis right across from mom's job. This time, I am not sure why, we had two other roommates besides living with my uncle and cousin; four men and three females crammed up in a three bedroom apartment. I have a pretty good hunch that this living arrangement was to make mom's financial situation less stressful. She did work long hours, but it was probably best to share an apartment with 4 men to make rent affordable rather than to struggle to support us here and my siblings and grandparents in Mexico.

Soon after we moved into that arrangement, school became my safe haven. Mom's roommates began to fondle me (never my uncle or cousin). I'm not sure if my sister suffered the same destiny. I never asked her. I never will. I remember being taken into their bedroom to relieve either one of them. One of those men is my mother's brother-in-law, the other man was a family 'friend'. What they both did to me was horrible. It was never intercourse, but they enjoyed themselves at my expense. After a while it was so 'normal' for me because it had been through it for so many years and with so many abusers that it did not faze me anymore. I was limp and terrified, but I never spoke about it.

My way out of the situation was accomplished by spending more and more time at school. I was safe there. I took on new activities; academic Olympics, school plays, and assignments that kept me away from home to avoid being molested. I now wonder if my sister was my replacement when I was gone. I hope not.

The abuse went on for many years, as I mentioned before it became a routine for them. I remember my mother's brother-in-law (our roommate) placing a 20 dollar bills on the table and offering them to me in return for allowing him to perform oral sex on me. I got 'smart' I would grab the 20 dollars and I would make him a new offer. "I will take the 20 dollars in return for not telling mom about what you have done to me." He never performed oral sex on me. A vile and disgusting human being; he is still alive. I see him occasionally. I held a grudge against him for decades. Recently, at a funeral I sat next to him at church.

During the entire service, my brain struggled with the idea of whether it was time to forgive him and letting that weight off my shoulders or if I should walk away to another pew to get away from him.

During a Catholic Mass, there is a time when you shake people's hands as a way to make peace with those around us. I was not looking forward to shaking his hand. My focus was not on listening to the service. It was with my mental struggle on whether or not I should be at peace with him. I begin to look for signs around church that would guide my thoughts away from my struggle. There was a large sign hanging from the ceiling that spoke about forgiveness. I read it and took a mental note of it; it was from Matthew 6:14-15, it read: *"For if you forgive other people when they sin against you, your heavenly Father will also forgive you. But if you do not forgive others their sins, your Father will not forgive your sins."* That was exactly what I needed. God had sent me the necessary words of encouragement to finally let go and forgive him for what he had done to me as a child. I felt such freedom and peace. I prayed for him. I still do. I pray that hopefully he has repented from all his sins and that he has not done what he did to me to anyone else.

I have forgiven him because holding a grudge against him only hurt me for years. I heard Joel Osteen say in one of his sermons that holding a grudge was like drinking poison and waiting for the other person to die. I was sick of slowly poisoning myself and I felt like a hypocrite every time I prayed *Our Father*. How could I ask God to forgive my offenses if I had not forgiven others myself? I read once that "The weak can never forgive. Forgiveness is the attribute of the strong." —Mahatma Gandhi. This quote is not an attempt to pat my own back, it is self-encouragement to remind myself that all these bad things have formed who I am and to remind me that my strength to forgive has helped me to become stronger. It is always a breath of fresh air to know that all things eventually come to an end; including bad situations.

This is what happened after years of abuse; it finally stopped. For a while, I lived a pretty 'normal' childhood and adolescence. We played kickball and hung outside during the summers. We ran under a giant water arch produced by a piece of 2 by 4 strategically placed in front of a water hydrant in the middle of our block. We lived in Little Village (a predominantly Mexican community in the city of Chicago) for many years. I had a good couple of years. Once more the calm before yet another storm.

Chapter 17: Mid-Teens

Puberty hit! I changed during my mid-teen years. I looked to find a reason, an excuse to why I made the choices I made at that time of my life. I wondered if my bad choices were due to the abuse I experienced, the situations I lived through, or the lack of a paternal figure. All of a sudden I became a rebel in search of a new and better life. I simply let my past define me.

Idiotically, I dropped out of school and married a controlling and abusive man a day short of my 18th birthday. In spite of the fact that I had seen signs of his abusive ways, I had fallen into the same cycle mom had been in with my father. I married him anyway. Although it was a hard marriage, a situation that made my life difficult; it also made me a stronger woman. A female who would never again be anyone's doormat. I had been one for too long. During the five years of marriage, I kept hoping that it would all change and we could have a 'normal' marriage. It was nothing but false hope.

I kept turning the other cheek for many years. Eventually, it was time to stop turning the cheek one more time. I learned that, yes, God said in Matthew 5:39; *"You have heard that it was said, 'Eye for eye and tooth for tooth.' But I tell you not to resist an evil person. If someone slaps you on your right cheek, turn to him the other also."* I learned that those lines never mentioned that God wants us to allow others to destroy us. Instead, it was a way to teach us to be forgiving of others even after they have abused us. That is exactly what I did. Although we shared an unhealthy relationship that lasted about 5 years, I forgave him and moved on.

After struggling to fix something that had no remedy, I left the relationship because after 5 long years, it was time to start a new and healthier chapter of my life. We were better people away from each other. I would lie if I said I was completely innocent in our relationship because, eventually, I resisted him and fought back, our relationship became mutual abuse.

It was for that reason that I decided to move away. It was time to move on before we could affect our daughter any further. We had to go our separate ways before we killed one another. This was yet again, another relationship that scarred me temporarily. I was afraid to be on my own. Afraid of life as a single parent. All those years of brainwashing had taken a toll on me. My mental status was defeated and I was drowning in a glass of water. I debated internally on whether or not I had made the right choice leaving his side. It took a long time for me to learn that I had made the right choice. It was hard in the beginning.

However, I have since learned from motivational speeches that we lose more when we let fear take control of our actions than what we would lose if we allowed courage to guide them. Moving away from that harsh situation was once again an opportunity to rise higher and to survive abuse one more time.

I learned that life is too short to be unhappy and that there is no reason why women have to live in an abusive relationship. It taught me to be stronger and less scared of men. Even though I learned to be stronger, years after my divorce there were times when my new partner would raise his hand or make an unexpected movement in close proximity to me when I would brace for impact. I was still scared. I thought that sooner or later my new partner would use physical abuse towards me. I was blemished, scared, scarred, and intimidated for many years. Deep down in my gut the fear remained for longer than I thought. I was intimidated by all men.

Ultimately, only God and time made me a stronger person. A person that began to run out of her car at the sight of a woman being abused to intervene. A person that defended other women and mentored them to move on and escape domestic violence. My marriage was without doubt a bad situation, but it was also a learning opportunity that pushed me beyond his expectations.

He thought that I would crumble up or hide in a corner; depressed, and feeling sorry for myself, but God had other plans for me. Plans to succeed and talk about my experiences to motivate and encourage others that have experienced similar situations to take a leap of faith and escape bad situations.

Despite our bad fallout, I consider my ex-husband to be my friend. After our separation, we communicated in order to be there for our two children. I never wished him bad in life. We share children and we had to be there for them. We continue to be civil with one another, but since our children are grown there is no need to maintain constant communication any longer. I wish him well in life. I hold no grudge against him. After all, we share one of God's greatest gifts, children, and we need to be there to support and guide them even through adulthood.

Chapter 18: Tragedy Strikes

After all I have been through in life, I am aware of the fact that life brings with it pain and suffering; we can find this documented in the Bible. God never promised his followers an easy life. In fact, he warned us to expect the opposite (**John 16:33**)—hardship and persecution from the world, and even correction from his own hand (**Hebrews 12:7**).

Unfortunately, the world would send hardship to my life once more. Just before separating from my ex-husband my life would get difficult once again. In those desperate moments, I did wonder what I had done wrong to deserve such unbearable pain. I wondered if I deserved the hand I was dealt. I had no answers at the moment and I was unable to reason why awful things happen to small children. It was not until adulthood that I learned about some possible answers to the why of hardship. I learned that there are three possible reasons for suffering; according to one of pastor Jeff Griffin's sermons, the three reasons for hardship are: natural consequences, divine intervention, and consequences to one's actions. Natural consequences refer to suffering in the world that IS caused by our fallen world. Divine intervention refers to times when God sees it necessary to intervene to guide us back to Him, and consequences to one's actions are pretty self-explanatory. The consequences we experience as the result of our actions. I can understand that marrying young and immature could bring negative consequences, but what about my childhood suffering? Is that a perfect example of our fallen world and therefore a result of natural consequences? Is it evil roaming in our lives? Is it divine intervention that causes childhood suffering? I have no answer for why life was sending another tragedy my way.

It was a cold winter morning and my abuser (husband) at that time was unable to care for our daughter, (chose not to take care of her) so I had to leave her under my cousin's care in order for me to go to work. I walked to their home and dropped my tiny four year old off at her house an early Saturday morning. Everyone was still asleep, so she sat down in their living room to watch TV until my cousin (babysitter) woke up. I worked all day and I picked my baby up later that evening. The night seemed normal, nothing unusual going on. My baby fell asleep on our way home, so I put her to bed as soon as we arrived home. The next day, I was off work and I was dressing my little girl when all of a sudden she said, "Mom, your cousin put his finger in my private." I have to admit, I did not know how to act, nor how to respond to her information. I hoped that it was all false, but how can a 4 year old make that up?

I began to find excuses to dismiss the situation. It was then that I recalled having had a conversation with my daughter and my young siblings about being cautious around him because he had exposed himself to one my sister just the week before. He worked at my mother's store which was located on the first floor of a two floor building. We lived upstairs. He had come up to use the washroom. He took care of his business and something more. As he was in the washroom he kept making strange noises; flicked the lights on and off, hummed, and cleared his throat. My little sister (early teenager) was in the living room just across from the washroom watching television. He continued to hum and make noises, all with the intention that my sister would turn and look at him. He finally succeeded; my sister turned to tell him to shut up and he showed her his penis.

My sister rushed downstairs to where mom was working to walk away from the situation, but never mentioned what my cousin had done to her. She later told my sisters and me about the incident. We felt a sense of urgency to communicate the incident with the younger children at home in order to prevent them from experiencing any abuse or exposure to his indecencies. We sat my little brother, nephew, and my daughter and told them, "Listen, if *Jose* does anything that makes you feel uncomfortable or tries to touch you in any way that makes you feel unsafe; you need to tell us immediately, understood?" We thought they understood, so we moved on.

As my daughter shared with me that he had touched her private, I thought it was a recall of what we had talked to them about earlier that week. I tried to make myself believe that. I couldn't handle the situation, so I let it go. I pushed it away. I was also scared of how my ex-husband would react to the situation. Would he blame me for it? Would I earn a beating if I told him what our child told me? I was already feeling guilty to begin with and not talking about it would be safer.

Just a few weeks later, another little girl in my family was fondled by my cousin, Jose. This time, he had gone too far. She had blood stains on her panties. Her mother called the police and as soon as my sister found out, she called me. I was at work when I received what I still categorized as one of the worst calls a mother can get. My sister was obviously very upset. Her voice trembled and I could hear and sense that she was holding back tears. "Vero, I'm afraid, I have bad news." "You need to take this calmly." she said.

"*Jose*, molested *Diana* and she is in the hospital as we speak." That means that what *Daisy* (my baby girl) told you about him is probably true." I was a mess. I had to ask my manager if I could go home, she agreed. When I got home, I held my little girl and asked her to share with me what she remembered from that horrible day. I needed to know what had happened at my cousin's house weeks before. She told me exactly what happened. *Jose* had taken her into his room while everyone else was sleeping. He played a song loud enough to keep any noises from escaping his room and he fondled her while he played with himself. I felt disgusted and enraged. Most of all, I felt guilty about what had happened to my cousin's daughter and for not acting promptly about what had happened to my little girl. I thought about how I could have spared another little girl from suffering the same faith that I had suffered years back. I felt guilty because I had lost the opportunity to show my daughter instant support when she was going through that situation. I had missed the opportunity to tell her how much I cared about her.

Nevertheless, it had all already happened and I had the opportunity to show her my love at that moment. After comforting my baby and telling her everything would be well, I did what I knew was the right thing to do. I called my cousin to try and comfort her and to lean on each other for support through that uncomfortable situation. She had already called the police and an investigation was well on its way.

In the meantime, I had to take my daughter to the hospital for a check-up to make sure she had no vaginal or anal tears. Unfortunately, weeks had passed since she was molested. She was physically well. Nevertheless, emotionally she would need counseling and care for a long time. I took her to Rainbows, an organization that is dedicated to being a support system for youth that has suffered loss, from death or trauma. They help children heal in a nurturing and resourceful environment. I know it helped her greatly, although she now shares that it made no positive difference because she didn't comprehend why she was receiving counseling in the first place. With time, she was able to forget all about the incident. It all became a repressed memory.

A year later or so, I had to testify against her abuser. It was one of the hardest things I had to do in my life. I stood before the jury to explain what my innocent child had shared with me about the incident. They handed me a teddy bear to use as a prop and model what my baby had gone through. I fell apart. A river of tears ran down my cheeks and my speech had lost clarity; my throat felt invaded by my heart's palpitations and I could not maintain my composure. The jurors' expressions were dysphoric and there was complete silence in the courtroom. I paused for a moment and tried my best to communicate with clarity what my baby had shared in regard to that horrific moment. When I was finally done speaking, one of the jurors said, "Off the record ma'am, you are one of the bravest women I have ever seen. I speak for all when I say that we all hope you heal and your little girl has a happy life." His words were relieving and heart-warming. His words embraced my soul and I felt that heavy weight lift off my shoulders. The verdict came soon; he was to serve 6 years at Cook County Jail. He would serve time for his crime.

That created lots of friction amongst my family. My mother was upset that I had 'put' my cousin in jail. She felt bad for her sister. I was angry because I could not understand why she felt bad for her sister and not for my little girl. My mother and I did not speak for a long time.

I remember her feeling sorry for him because his Thanksgiving dinner in jail was a hotdog and we were having a traditional turkey dinner. I had no remorse. I did not feel responsible for what he was going through. He put himself in jail! It was the consequence to his actions that condemned him. I was glad he was away from other little girls.

Eventually, he was freed, but he was deported to Mexico due to his crimes. He could no longer become a legal citizen of the United States,

something else I was blamed for. I knew it was not

my fault. I have a clear conscious. I am not sure if I

am still seen as the cause for his consequences, but I

don't lose any sleep over it.

Chapter 19: My Little Girl

As for my daughter; she is well presently. She has her own family; two children and a third child on the way. She's had some struggles, but life has taught her to strive to survive. I do know that this affected her emotionally, but she has put it in the past and does not dwell on it. She knows about it now because one of my sister told her of the incident during her teen years. My daughter had no recollection of the event. I still wish she wouldn't have found out about it, but she did and nothing can change that. My sister did not mean to cause any pain when she shared what had happened to her. It was a spur of the moment kind of a thing.

My daughter was not allowed to go to my aunt's house and my daughter never understood the reason behind it. My sister thought it was appropriate to share the incident with my daughter. She was surprised to find out that she didn't remember the incident. My daughter did ask me about the situation and I shared with her that I did not want her to relive the moment, so I had kept it hidden from her all those years. She deserved to be happy. She deserves to be happy.

She has a great heart and knows God has always been by her side. I pray that she lives a joyous, fulfilled life. A life of forgiveness, yet a life with the assertiveness to know how special and unique she is in order to never accept abuse from anyone.

It has been over 20 years since this incident and I have forgiven my cousin for his cruelty against us, but it is still difficult to imagine how I would react the day I see him face to face again. I will not know how to address him. It is too hard to let go when he has never demonstrated remorse. He has never apologized. On the contrary, he once mentioned that he didn't understand why I had not forgiven him yet. I hope he's had the time to repent about his offenses and that he never does it again. I fear for his own children. Hopefully, he never goes through what he caused us to go through. I know God has forgiven him and I don't wish bad upon him. But he will never know to what extent his actions affected our family.

His actions caused us lots of pain. It was this incident that brought back my repressed memories. It all came back to me like a flashback. Just like a derailed locomotive. My brain had hidden that memory from me for so many years and it came back to light as it had just occurred. My daughter's incident took me back to the past; I was a helpless and innocent 7 year old. I remember why mom and dad fought so angrily the day before we left my birthplace. *I remembered being in the bedroom with my father, him laid me next to him on the cot, grabbed my little hand and pulled it towards his aroused private. I recall him not holding back the inappropriateness of having me touch him. I remember my helpless and unsuccessful attempt to pull my little hand back away from him. I can visualize it now playing in my head, just like I can play a video on my camera, the memory is back in my head. My poor mother walked into the room and fortunately my father was busted.* I am not sure if he had done this before. I am not sure if he did other things to me. I often wonder if I will ever recall any other incidents. I hope not.

During some time, I faked sexual acts with my little friends and their toys growing up. How can a seven year old know about sex? Considering that we had no television, no technology, no access to any adult content, with no way to learn about sexuality, something else had exposed me to it. I still wonder if he had molested me before this happened, but I do not have the answers to that, just as I don't have recollection of so many other memories.

It is probably good to have it remain as dissociative amnesia; the inability to recall autobiographical information as a way to protect me from remembering the trauma I was put through. I have also forgiven my father for his offenses against me, my mother, and my siblings and I often wonder if he forgave himself. I think about whether or not he had a recollection of all the damage he caused us. I didn't see my father for over a year after we left Mexicali. Then one day, he showed up to my grandparents' town. I remember being so scared to know that he was near. I felt nauseated and trembled like a leaf on a windy day. The thought of seeing him was terrifying. I could not control my fear. I decided that my brother and I would hide in the large tree in front of our house.

It was summer and the tree was abundant with green, shiny leaves. It was perfect for hiding. We climbed as high as we could and sat between thick branches. We remained completely silent for what seemed to be a long time. We could hear grandma calling our names in a grumpy and impatient tone, louder and louder as she became more and more agitated. We remained motionless. After a long while, my brother had to urinate. I asked him to hold it for a little while longer, but it got to the point when he couldn't hold it any longer. "I hadn't thought this through," I thought. If he peed from on top of the tree, she would notice it immediately. Trees do not perspire a single stream of yellow liquid. We had to descend from our hiding place. It was inevitable; we would eventually see my father again.

We climbed down and I hoped it was too late to go visit my dad, but as soon as my grandmother saw us, she hurried us out the door. The town was no more than fifteen by fifteen streets large, so we arrived to where he was staying within minutes. We hid behind grandma's skirt and shook like gelatin at sight of our father. I don't recall if he greeted us, kissed, or hugged us. I have no recollection of any affectionate treatment. I just remember him sitting across from us in a large room. I remember being scared, nothing else. Our visit was brief and strange. We did not see him again for about 3 years. Mom was the only one who heard from him often. His threats and false accusations haunted my mother even 2500 miles apart, she felt threatened by him for many years. I learned from her a saying, "el valiente dura hasta que el cobarde quiere." which means the brave endures until the coward allows it. I still remember this and keep it close to my heart, to remind myself to never be a coward for any one. That's what she did, the brave ended when she decided to no longer be the coward. She was sick of him threatening with taking us away and accusing her of being an unfit mother. She was so sick of it that she eventually said, "Fine come take your kids!" That's all he needed to hear, a determined, brave woman that did not fear losing her kids. He stopped threatening and did not bother mom again.

Chapter 20: The Second Visit

I had a second chance to see my father here in the United States. My tenth birthday arrived and so did my father. He resided in California with his new girlfriend, but I guess he had decided to come see us for the first time here in the United States. I was not afraid to visit him this time, perhaps because he was visiting us at my aunt's house (his sister). An aunt that had always taken care of us as she cared for her own. We spent most weekends with her and we always felt welcomed and safe with her.

With her, we had family get togethers at Cermak Pool, a fun place to swim, play and barbecue. I remember going there and paying ten cents to go into the pool. We would get a wire basket and a numbered safety pin to claim our belongings. I loved that place! We were able to play and barbecue with my dad during his first visit with us here in Chicago. It was fun. After a day of softball, swimming, and barbecuing, the following day, he took us shopping. I recall what he bought for me; a pair of sandals, a dress and a doll head with a mini-blow dryer, plastic rollers, and fake make up. I was very happy. So happy that I went home and told my mother, "You know mom, my dad is not such a bad person anymore." She remembers shivering and her skin becoming filled with goose bumps as she heard me say that. She has never forgotten the moment I shared that with her. Sometimes, she still mentions it and shared that she wanted more than anything for it to be true, but during that time, he was still threatening with taking us away from her, so she knew it was all a facade. Despite it all, he was good to us that time. He celebrated my birthday and bought me a cake. I still have a picture of that day (included). This is the one of the three positive memories I have of him.

Another happy memory was from a very long time before. It is a very short memory. The only memory I have of my early years now that I think about it. I must have been 5 or 6 years old, we went to Mazatlán, Mexico and I remember sleeping in a beautiful hotel room, by the beach in a tall building with an elevator. We woke up early one morning and took the elevator to get down to the lobby. We were all in the elevator and I remember him pushing the button to go downstairs, telling us that we are going to Durango (my mom's town) quite a distance away. We were almost instantly down to the first floor, and I believed we were at my mother's town. We walked to a nearby seafood restaurant. I don't remember what I ate, but I remember my little sister had a shrimp cocktail. I remember her red cheeks and the happiness on her face as she savoured giant shrimp. I don't remember anything else from that day. However, it was a day with smiles, food, and no abuse, another happy day to cherish forever.

Chapter 21: Bright Colors

Back home with mom in Little Village, years went passed and mom continued to be our father and mother. I didn't hear from my father for a long time. Then just one other time after my 10th birthday celebration, I received a gift from him; jewelry and a promise to come celebrate my 15th birthday in 1987. I had not seen him since my 10th birthday celebration but I was looking forward to seeing him again.

Suddenly, on a warm spring day, May 5, 1986, a day that started as any other day, a Monday school day. The day started as usual, but things began heading south promptly. Despite it being my birthday, there was nothing really special about it. I was a year away from my quinceñera and from seeing my father again. I was thrilled about a quinceñera, but the quinceñera celebration never came.

On my birthday, May 5th, yes, cinco de mayo, not Mexican Independence Day, but the commemoration of a battle in Puebla, Mexico between a much larger French army which was defeated by the Mexicans back in 1862. Fast forwarding to May 5th, 1986, that day, we were picked up from school for an early dismissal. Mom worked long hours, and never picked us up early from school, but on that May day, she did. She picked us up early and it seemed as if she was nervous and had been crying. She drove us back to her business (she had a bridal shop for almost 25 years). Once we were there, she gave me money and instructed me to go buy a couple of outfits. I thought nothing of it. It was my birthday and she always gave us money to go shopping. Her bridal shop was one of many businesses down 26th street commerce, so there were plenty of stores to shop for an outfit. She said we were going to visit my father because he had been shot and was very sick. We were traveling with my dad's sister, I had dismissed the part where she shared that he was very sick and I was super excited about visiting my dad in California. I hoped that he would get well soon and hopefully take us to Disneyland (I was still just a kid). I went to the store and purchased some cute outfits (bright canary yellow and hot pink). It was the Cyndi Lauper years so it was the style. Mom took one look at my outfits and said, "I think you need to find a dark color, maybe a black outfit, just in case your dad doesn't make it." Despite the history with my dad, I prayed that he would get well, but I listened to my mother and I went back to the store and bought myself a black outfit. We left immediately that evening. The entire flight there, I prayed that God would heal my father and that we had time to catch up with him. The flight seemed to take forever. When we arrived, we were picked up by another one of my dad's sisters. She seemed sad, but she was happy to see my sister and me. We were eager to go see him at the hospital, but they told us no children were allowed in the hospital.

My aunts were also expecting their mother (my paternal grandmother) to arrive from Yuma, Arizona so we could not leave the house. Yet, another reason for why we could not go see my dad at the hospital.

Chapter 22: Cold and Motionless

I was somewhat confused when grandma arrived to my aunt's house. According to my mother, my dad had been shot. When my grandmother walked into my aunt's house the first thing she asked was, "Did they catch the guy that ran him over? I was confused because there were two different versions of what had happened to my dad. When she asked about it, my aunts were motionless and speechless. They saw the confusion in my eyes. I still hoped that whatever the cause was, he would be well. Grandma persevered, she asked my aunts one more time and before a word came out of their mouths; my grandmother began to scream, "My son is dead, isn't he?!" My aunts were both trying to calm her down and explain that he was in the hospital, but that visiting times were over. Grandma kept pushing them to tell her the truth and one of my aunts broke the news to he; to us. "Yes, mom, he is dead; I'm sorry" she muttered." She began to cry and scream like a baby. My sister and I could not contain ourselves and balled our eyes out. How could it be? We were supposed to catch up. We were supposed to spend time with him, to talk with him and mend our father-daughter relationship. My prayers were unanswered. My father had died. I had no chance to talk to him, to reconcile, to tell him I loved him no matter what.

The next time I saw him, he was motionless, cold, and silent. He was in his coffin. One of the worst places to see your loved ones; a funeral. He was very different from the man I remembered. His face was expressionless, a straight mouth with no smile, his skin looked purplish, and he was cold to the touch like a Chicago winter night. I felt as if half my soul was destroyed or gone with him. It is an unexplainable feeling, I felt as if I had lost half my identity. I felt numb and empty.

After the service, I remember his abuse. Not the sexual abuse, just the beating. I wondered if he played all these memories in his head as he lost his battle with death. However, I held no grudges against him, after all he was my father and it was not my job to judge him. He left many unanswered questions, doubts, and countless possibilities; the possibility to tell him I forgave him. The possibility of telling him I loved him and of hearing him say that he loved me. The possibility of him apologizing and expressing his sincere remorse for what he had done to us in the past.

He also left behind so many opportunities; the opportunity to meet his grandchildren and to try to be a great and normal grandfather. The opportunity to age (he was 33 when he died). The opportunity to LIVE.

Chapter 23: The Unanswered

Sometimes, I still wonder what our lives would have been if he was around. Would we have had the opportunity to reconcile? I know for a fact that he would have never been part of my mother's life, but I believe that we would've had the opportunity to rebuild our father-daughter relationship. That opportunity was also forever lost. I know this sounds like false hope, but with God all is possible and hope and faith can mend all things.

Sometimes, I am saddened about many things that happened to me throughout my life, but the one that saddens me the most is not having the opportunity to sit and talk with him as an adult, to share what our lives had been like while we were apart. I know he knows that I have forgiven him, but it is not the same than to have the opportunity to tell him face to face. I have been silent for many years, about many things, but losing the opportunity to dialogue with someone that has gone to a better place makes me feel impotent.

However, all my past sadness has been replaced with happiness and hope through the understanding that God will allow all of us the opportunity to see one another at the end of times to have closure and answers for all unanswered and unsolved situations. I am thankful and happy for being alive and well despite all the traumatic experiences I lived through; I am here. I survived.

I am happy to see a new day and observe the beauty that surrounds us; the sun, stars, moon, trees, squirrels; nature. I am forever grateful to have the possibility to tell my story and hopeful that I will inspire someone to come out of the shadows and be a victor not a victim. My heart is full of joy and hope.

I made it. I lived to tell my story. A story that I am sure many others have lived or still are living through. A story that may guide those who remain silent to speak up and be silent no more.

My hope is that those who have lived through similar situations see themselves in my story, just as I saw myself in other literature. I hope they rise out of the shadows and understand how important they are. Hopefully, my story will give them the hope they need to escape abuse, from being deprived of their freedom and choice. I know that just like I did, many live a secret and silent past.

Some remain quiet to avoid throwing others under the bus; perhaps, their own brother, father, uncle, aunt, or cousin. It is time to speak up and shake off the fear. Time to get rid of what is keeping you from your potential. Rise and shine. Shake it off and live a life of victory.

Not many know about my past and for those who read about it; sadness is probably an inevitable emotion, because no one likes to learn about children suffering. However, this is not a sad story. It is a story about learning, surviving, and making the best out of bad situations. According to some studies, I should have been a gangbanger, drug addict, a failure in society; everything pointed me towards that direction, but I decided that the only way out was God and education. No study, statistic, or generalization can influence me without my permission. I knew that other studies showed that education could be the key to success for many, so I went back to school to better my chances of making it in the world.

That is exactly what I did. I went back to school immediately after my separation from my then abusive husband. I had to better myself educationally, spiritually, and emotionally; books kept me busy and sane. They were my escape to a place of peace and safety. I remember finding a book in the LRC at Richard J. Daley College that helped to change my life. I don't recall the exact name, but it was close to the following: *Battered Women and the Men they Love.* By reading that book, I learned for the first time that I was not the only woman in a domestic violent situation. I learned that no matter what level in the social hierarchy women belonged to many are abused; doctors, lawyers, teachers, from all backgrounds, and races. Domestic violence does not discriminate against, creed, color, social class, nor educational level. Women all around the globe suffer at the hands of their boyfriends, husbands, or their significant others.

Chapter 24: The Power of Books

Before reading books and for a very long time, I believed that all women were abused. I thought it was the norm. It was not until I separated from my ex-husband that I figured out that the way my mother and I were treated was not acceptable and that not everyone experienced abuse. However, I never thought that educated, professional women were abused. I did think that domestic abuse was the norm in my case.

Perhaps, norm isn't the correct word to use to describe domestic violence, but unfortunately that is the most accurate way to describe it.

Each day, women die at the hands of those who are supposed to love and protect them; their significant others. These are men that take the "until death do us part" phrase to extreme levels.

I learned so much from books, I used them for self-healing; a process I still continue to pursue. I navigated through the numerous rows of organized books in the library. The scent of books in the library gave me a sense of peace and healing. Books gave me the peace and quiet I needed to heal from my past, as well as the strength and the knowledge to keep fighting to make it in life.

` Once again, just like during my childhood, school had become my safe haven; a place to meditate, learn, grow, and become stronger. Every achievement became a personal reward. Rewards that helped to heal every bad memory from my past. Self-therapy was accomplishable through the literature I read.

However, this worked temporarily and it helped me to externally wear a plastic smile. Self-therapy helped me to become cautious and to over analyze situations. It prevented me from trusting anyone or anything. On the other hand, it also made me assertive, organized, and persevering. Deep inside, I had insecurities and I gave people too much power. Sometimes, I still do.

I give power to those who show no kindness towards me. Those who dislike me or think little of me. The scared and scarred child still lives inside this woman's body. Despite that, I continue the self-healing process, because although, I have come a long way, I have not learned to let things that hurt me slide. Life has been difficult for me but I try to remember the personal and professional growth I have made to encourage myself to stop allowing others to make me doubt my worth. I try to remind myself how far I have come despite the hardship...not to pat myself on the back, but to remind myself that I am a victor and not a victim. Understanding this keeps me on my toes. It reminds me that I should never allow anyone else to victimize me.

I now understand that we are the only ones responsible for allowing pain and suffering in our lives, if we do not allow it, pain and suffering will not affect us. I allowed it for many years. I now often remind myself to walk with my forehead high, with a genuine smile on my face; a real smile. A smile of appreciation for who I am and who I have become despite all hardship. It is very important for me to wear a genuine smile. I had lost it many years ago and sometimes stumble upon sorrow once in a while, but I bounce right back to the happy person I am and will continue to be.

Chapter 25: Choices

Life gives us the opportunity to make our own choices. Just like most human beings, I have made some good and some bad choices. However, I have always been alcohol and drug free. I never did anything I would regret later. Related to drugs that is. I did, however, drop out of school and got pregnant. I never regretted my pregnancy. Having a baby brought happiness to my life. I remember seeing her little face for the first time; seeing her make a gesture that showed her perfect, pea size dimples, her rosy cheeks, and her fine golden hair made me smile. My little girl was such a wonderful gift. A new reason to strive to do my best. Having a child was not a mistake.

On the other hand, dropping out of high school was a stupid decision. It would push me to live in poverty once again. It seemed to be a curse that followed me just as abuse did.

However, I worked my butt off to make ends meet and raise my children as best as I could. My goals was to give them all I never had. I think, I did a pretty good job. I lived a life of limitations, but I had the essentials; a roof over our heads, food, and a job. I struggled for a while. However, God made amazing changes in my life. There are no limits to what He can do.

I am now what you call a bookworm; I take no offense to that fact. Books have helped me to heal, learn new things; topics that I otherwise would ignore, and they have helped me to broaden my understanding of life. Books also gave me the knowledge I now utilize in my current position. Being a bookworm has enriched my life more than you can ever imagine.

I was not always a bookworm. For many years, I struggled with reading comprehension. I went back and forth across lines of text without understanding a single phrase. All of the words melted together and nothing made sense. I went through schooling year after year without understanding what I read. Reading was very frustrating. I never read for pleasure, but I would force myself through assigned texts to maintain my grade point average. I went through this difficulty through high school. It was not until my college years that Dr. Kennedy helped me to identify ways to improve my reading skills. It finally all made sense.

She indirectly helped me to create self-help tools to chunk the texts as she taught me reading strategies to help my students. I was able to use these new tools and strategies to comprehend the texts I read. Those tools helped me to avoid the distraction that an entire page full of words caused my brain. It was then that I began to read books for pleasure. I could not put books down. I wanted to get to the end to find out what happened; how the stories ended. I read books with better fluency and improved comprehension. I was glad that reading was no longer a dreadful task, instead, it was a new way to discover new learning opportunities. I often wondered when it was that I learned how to read as a child, but I still can't remember.

I have vague memories of what I read as a pre-teen and as a teen. I remember reading gossip magazines such as People and Tv Novelas, short articles in the Spanish newspaper, and song lyrics from CD inserts. I don't ever remember reading any novels. It was easier for me to understand short informational texts. I don't remember reading academic texts before my teen years. Today, I read every day with no problem.

We all have a story and the events in our story mold who we become, but I strongly believe that God has predetermined our paths and we affect the path we continue through our decisions. We choose to follow a path with God or a path without Him. I have done both. There were many times when I walked my path away from Him, sometimes I still do. Sometimes, I still want to negotiate with Him to do my own will. However, he helps me just as He helps all of us to redirect our paths.

In life, we will always have the capability to blame other for our own choices. Life has taught me that I cannot blame anyone for my decisions. Blaming others is easy, but we have the ability to make our own choice and to make changes in our lives, therefore even if we are influenced by others the decision for our actions are ultimately our choices.

If I would have turned out to be an abuser, it would have been my decision and not my father's fault. It is our responsibility to change any generational curse; we need to learn to overcome our dysfunctions. God created us to overcome issues by making our own decisions.

There are many things that we assimilate to from our past experiences and no matter how hard we try there are things that we cannot get away from. Even after surviving hardship and reaching success, a difficult past can continue to affect our present. It does not matter how strong we appear to be; a bad past can influence our present. It is true that what we see modeled growing up may cause confusion in our lives, but even then, we can make a different choice. Make a positive change in your life. Forgive those who have hurt us. All of this while not allowing others to belittle us. Choose to shine and live your life without letting a negative past sour your path, impede your success, stall or stop you from reaching your highest potential; your purpose in life.

Chapter 26: Still Self-healing

I have worked on self-healing for the past 40 years, as you read, life threw me a few curveballs. Despite this, I have always made my best effort to remain positive and strive to overcome adversity. My goals have also always been to be caring, compassionate and loving towards others.

Unfortunately, doing so has caused me pain.

My naivetés or lack of experience and giving everyone the benefit of the doubt has proved to be the wrong thing to do when trusting others. Not everyone is genuine or always out to do well. Many people that crossed my path used and abused my kindness. I hold no grudges to that fact, but life has taught me to be alert and aware of others' true intentions. That's a good thing!

Throughout my path to healing from the evil that was done to me. I was never deterred from my purpose. No matter what difficulties I faced, I continued to do good for people, sometimes through self-sacrifice, but with the understanding of the importance to do well without reservation and to treat others like I wanted to be treated. I see that as my given purpose in life. The reason for being here despite all hardship.

Luckily for me, just as there were bad people in my life there were also many others that were gifts and blessings for me. I see them as compensation for my distraught past. I have been very lucky to come across people in my life that believed in me and pushed me beyond my comfort zone which, in return, pushed me away from mediocrity. Yes, there were times in my life when I felt compelled to fall into self-pity, but God sent constant reminders that pushed me to shine and come out from the shadows.

Most of those reminders were people that pushed me away from falling back into recalling the past and feeling sorry for myself. Pity that would have pushed me into a world filled with excuses, with no purpose, nor drive to change the status quo. Doing so would have made me a casualty and that was not something I was willing to be.

I learned that doubting myself would keep me from my success from the future that God had in store for me. I could not let my past ruin my future; my purpose in life. I believe that one of my duties is to be the light to others' darkness, or, at least, I hoped I would be. I want to stop the cycles of pain and suffering for others by sharing my story. I want to change the world. I know that seems impossible, but even if I can make a positive change for one person, I would feel accomplished.

I live by the belief that kindness creates ripple effects that inevitably touch many people and that by doing so, it helps to change my own past into a positive outcome. I am not going to let what happened to me define me negatively. I want to remember the child I was as a memory of why I strive to do my best for myself and others each and every day. My hope is that by speaking up about my past, I can help others that experienced similar situations to come out of the shadows if they have not done so. I hope for them to come out and heal to help others do the same.

I share my story knowing that I will probably suffer repercussions from my own family members when they identify some of the perpetrators in my story, but if my story can help one person, it will be all worth it.

Chapter 27: Unveiling Truths

While adding the finishing touches to my
story, one of my sister asked if she could read my
story. I share it with her. She has been concerned
about me publishing without having a talk with mom.
She feels very strongly that mom should know
everything I remember. That she should find out
through me that I remember the sexual abuse and not
by a third party or from the book. The day after I
shared my book with her; her response to my book
shocked me. I didn't know how many things she
knew that I did not know. She shared that mom and
she had a recent conversation while on a short
getaway. Mom shared with her that while she lived
with my father, her mother went to visit us in
Mexicali and she had noticed how bad our situation
there really was. My grandmother was very attached

to our brother so she decided to take him back to La Joya (not before asking my dad). Once my little sister realized that grandma was taking our brother, she insisted on going too. So Grandma went to ask my dad if she could take them both and his response was "A ese se lo doy por dos años y a la otra se la regaló." He let them go.

During that visit, mom told grandma that she was thinking of leaving my dad and going somewhere far where no one could find us. Since grandma was concerned about mom's plans, she went back home and told grandpa what mom was planning. Grandpa wrote her a letter telling her not to disappear, that she was welcome back with all of us. My grandpa also wrote my dad a very serious letter, but we don't have any details about it. My sister also shared other facts that may point to why my dad was so aggressive towards us. Mom was madly in love with another man. She married my father out of spite. She was heartbroken because the man of her dreams had unexpectedly impregnated another woman. She thought she could get back at that guy by going off with the next guy and getting married. Unfortunately, mom's consequences to her actions were horrible. Her suffering was much worse.

Mom was young and he was not her first choice which may mean several things; maybe dad thought, "okay, maybe this girl really loves me or here is my opportunity to have a real family." However, I'm sure he was a smart man and if he didn't realize it early on, maybe after sometime he realized the truth and it must have hurt him, his ego, su hombría. It's still not a justification for him abusing any of us.

Although, if he really loved mom, finding out about mom not loving him turned his sentiment towards her into hate.

I am not sure why they stayed in a relationship like that when he could have easily ended the marriage. Unless, again, his ego or maybe his hope for a family was so important to him that even if it was a facade, he remained in it.

My sister shares; "I think his actions were a combination of things. Usually the common denominator for people that commit horrible acts when they are adults has to do with their upbringing. He was probably bullied endlessly which probably why he became a boxer in order to protect himself. He needed help and he probably never got it. If he was abused, he would never tell anyone. Most men never do."

Mom shared with my sister about the day she decided to leave him. My sister was very inquisitive and asked mom about what made her finally have the courage to leave him? She never thought she would confirm my story. She told her that one day she discovered my dad sexually abusing me. She said she saw it with her own eyes... por una rendija de la recámara. (through a crack in the bedroom wall). She said she lost it and that she yelled at him and told him que era peor que un cerdo (he was worse than a pig). She said that was it. She told him that she was leaving and that all she wanted from him was money for the bus and that he would never see us again.

At that point in time, my sister remembered my flashbacks, She told mom, I remembered. Mom said, -mi pobre Vero, la pelea fue tan fuerte que no se si ella se acuerda." (My poor child, the fight was so horrible, that I didn't think she remembered).

My sister said, "Si mami, Vero se acuerda". Mom, could not believe I remembered, so she asked my sister one more time, ¿De verdad se acuerda?" (Does she really remembers?) My sister confirmed it once more. "Yes mom, she remembers."

Mom was unsure if I did and like me with my own daughter, she did not want to ask me to avoid hurting me by reminding me about it. It was best to leave it buried if I did not remember.

Which is why my sister thinks it will do both of us good to talk about it and put it in the past.

Chapter 28: 40 Years Later

After sharing my book with my sister, I found out many things that I was not expecting. Some of them, I had briefly heard about in the past, but never did question them. I didn't have the courage to listen to one more detail. Yet, finding out about these new details pushed me to the sudden choice of going back to my birthplace to find closure and finally let go of all that trash to fully heal. At least, that's what I hoped for.

I went back. I was there for a few hours. Nothing has changed in that old town. The only thing that has changed is my age. I walked away when I was 7 and walked back in at 45. The roads are the same, the house is the same; even the school walls are lime green with white windows. The ground is still parched and inhibited with poverty. It felt as if I had left the day before.

I am not sure if going there changed anything for me. I still feel hollow at times, empty and with such an uncertainty about why my father was the way he was. I know that my past will never affect me negatively. My life will never shatter. I am a person with a clear purpose. I am centered and I have made up my mind that with God all things are possible. I have picked up that pieces and no matter how many times I fall, I know how to pick and dust myself off to keep going. God is my strength and my guide. With Him, I will always triumph.

Our past has the potential to affects us positively and negatively, but when we understand our purpose for being, we will always stay positive. We all have a purpose. Find yours and walk towards it to live to your highest potential and impact our world with one act of kindness at a time.

ABOUT THE AUTHOR

Veronica Zamora-Loera is an award winning
educator; named Teacher of the Year in 2015,
someone who identifies herself through the phrase,
"what you see is what you get." A woman with deep
but healed scars. A person who dreams of touching
lives positively with her story. Someone who always
has a smile on her face and makes every effort to
cheer someone up by giving a genuine compliments.
A mother, wife, sister and daughter. A new author.

The Second Visit: My tenth birthday surrounded by
my cousins, my brother and my father.

My paternal grandmother; our only angel.

The baseball field; where I last looked out a car's

window to wave goodbye to my father.

My mother and siblings near

Durango, Mexico.

Back to my birth place after almost 40 years;

2018.

With my sister; my moral support and strength.

My old home; the street I remembered so clearly.

The home I grew up in.

The school I remember little about. I could not get myself to get out of the car to take a picture.

The cotton fields.

94111215R00105

Made in the USA
Lexington, KY
25 July 2018